GET
"On The Good Foot"
AMERICA

REV. DR. LISA C. TOWNSEND

Get "On The Good Foot"

COPYRIGHT 2020 by **Rev. Dr. Lisa C. Townsend**

ISBN: 978-0-692-77482-3

Printed in the United States of America

Rev. Dr. Lisa C. Townsend

GET "ON THE GOOD FOOT" . . .

A Spiritual & Practical Guide Book to Solutions for Social Issues & Racial Injustices: Keys to Social Justice, Advocacy, ...

Come on America! UNITE, Pull Up Your Bootstraps! Turn This Country Around! & Get On "Good" Footing.

WITH A LOOK AT ROLE POLICY & RELIGION PLAYS IN FIGHT FOR UNITY AND EQUALITY FOR ALL

He Picked Me up, Out of A Miry Pit,
Placed My Feet on Solid Footing

—Psalm 40:2

CONTENTS

PREFACE

The Good Foot Definition

The Good Foot: RESET. To begin a task. Slang. Get oneself, One's rear in gear. Get whatever it is one's doing, Betta "Get It Together" on solid footing. Get, Get, Get... on a solid foundation, & FAST! With police brutality of African Americans on the rise, over the last 4 yrs, there's been great racial disparities in shootings of African Americans in the U.S. A total of 429 civilians shot, 88 of whom were Black, as of June 4, 2020, according Statistia. The rate of loss of lives from fatal police shootings have been higher than any other ethnicity. Loss of lives this year, after June 4, 2020 totals, 135 deaths, 164 deaths in the first 8 months, and the numbers continue to rise because of it. That's when I think of singer, James Brown, during the civil rights era, urging us in his 70's funk inspiring song, energizing the people "To Get on The Good Foot!

Ringing In the back of my mind, I also hear the voice of the prince of civil rights, (I call him) Congressman John Lewis Sounding the Alarm, that it's time To Get In Some Good Trouble.

Even young, millennium African Americans need to know there's no time to rest on the hard work of our forefathers in the movement.

We must be ready & woke. That means watch our backs, our steps, with more attention to our behaviors & unjust repercussions for one's actions, errors, more than ever. But more so, attention to policies, and the change of them than ever. It is apparent, once again the country is slipping in more ways than we could imagine, & it's repeating its past, and divided against itself...but now, a silent, invisible enemy has arrived on the scene. Waging war against us, all while we fight against one another and see our fellow countrymen as our enemy & real threat, COVID-19 is its name.

The Corona Virus disease of 2019. Written during the onset of COVID-19, A time of reflection. 2020. An Election Year. We weren't just experiencing COVID, but what I describe as a Tsunami of pandemics. Police brutality & criminal justice leading the pack, having to close my practice for the health & safety of others, and myself. I didn't even have a surgical mask to my name, which was being recommended, let alone any type of mask-period. Reality had set in. Things have gotten really real. It's time, to "Get On The Good Foot".

INTRODUCTION

GET ON THE GOOD FOOT...AMERICA
PULL UP YOUR BOOTSTRAPS & GET ONE'S
FOOTING HEADED IN A DIFFERENT
DIRECTION.

When I was a little girl, in the 70's. My parents
had James brown on heavy rotation at our home.
He TOLD US TO SAY IT LOUD, I'M Black &
I'm Proud (1968) and Get On The Good Foot
(1972). I would sit out on my front porch and
sing; Say, It Loud, I'm Black & I'm Proud. My
mom joked that before I understood what I was
singing, I would say, "I'm Black & I'm Brown.
Well, once I mastered this anthem of love,
dignity & pride in who I was during a time of
cultural embracement, I graduated to Get on
the Good Foot. It did just what it set out to do.
The groove soulful & energetic, got me moving.
Pumped, to get at it. Do something purposeful.
The definition of the Good Foot was a slang
word used to urge one to get off on the right
start. begin, pronto, get moving, cracking/

or crack'in. Get one's butt in gear. Time's a-wast'in. As I began to study this song and the significance of its words, I discovered that Mr. Brown not only told us to "Get On The Good Foot", but then he instructed us...And "Do the Bad Thang." "Bad", as in "Good." The tough thing. Just as congressman Lewis & his urging of people to STAND UP FOR WHAT'S RIGHT, TAKE ACTION. GET INTO SOME "GOOD"-NECESSARY TROUBLE. America was now needing to dig in deep, regain its footing, step up its game, stabilize it's foundation, & PRONTO!

There was the realization that our feet, the foundation we we're standing on, was not solid & we were now standing on shaky ground. The country was spiraling out of control & lost its focus and footing, being distracted by a Tsunami of divides. Protest are breaking out from fatal shootings of African Americans. Looting, Deaths from Covid, Grief & Loss, Mental Illness at an all-time high with anxieties, substance abuse, and PTSD. Lo & behold, now, trying to gain its footing & gear up to fight this invisible enemy, a Pandemic, it knows little about, America is in a war on its own soil, not with other countries, but with its own fellow Americans. Again, Lo & behold we are in a fight with an invisible enemy, but one we know little to nothing about. It's time for America to put on its combat boots for war, pull up its bootstraps & Get On The Good Foot & in a hurry, decide to reconcile our differences in this country, turn it around, & head in a different direction. After all, how long must this country fight over the same inequality & injustice issues, continue this insanity?

Unfortunately, the problems we're facing in the country are not new. We need to make change, change in leadership, starting with the presidency, Joseph Robinette Biden Jr.

This book will outline the areas where the U.S. has been weakened historically, with divisiveness/ distractions & loss of focus such as spirituality/ religion, politics, racism, attacks on democracy and take the steps to unite and correct those integral missteps.

We will explore what's at the root? If It's Supremacy or Superiority? Do we realize that the war on African Americans or any other American to prove one's supremacy or superiority is a losing battle? Furthermore, every time the country does it, we get off on the wrong footing, & there is much at stake. The economy, healthcare, voter suppression, the national security, health and safety of All Americans. There are too many unjust actions being taken, and some Americans are too busy stirring up bad trouble, for real, literally, for the country that they aren't able to contemplate the price that will have to be suffered because of it.

All people. As Vice President to former President Barack Obama, Joe Biden says in his race for the 2020 presidency, "We are fighting for the soul of the nation." My purpose also is to reveal the deceptions, misconceptions, perceptions & raise consciousness of the price every American pay, when prejudice, racism, & division is at the root of our issues. There's a saying that says small minds worry about other people. Big minds focus on solving problems, not stirring them up for others, or cause division. Those are signs of a fearful & weak person let alone a Leader. What's at stake for All of us?

Let's Get To The Heart Of The Matter! By Increasing the dialogue & discussions on prejudice, racism, inferiority complexes, crab mentality. Question the mindset, ask yourselves- Where Do they come from? The mindsets, belief systems, & heal them.

Learn how to fact check, diversify & associate

with those different from yourselves, read from various outlets, (note: Isolation enemy of unity), check out all news sources, reality test. Pull up our big men & women pants, "Get on The Good Foot"- Solid ground, in uniting this country. Included, in chapters ahead will be actions that average, every day, hardworking individuals can do to change our country on various levels of advocacy & change. Unfortunately, the problems we're facing in the country is not new. We need to make change, & change in leadership, starting with the presidency. Joseph Robinette Biden Jr. He's not perfect, but he knows pain, which is universal. America needs to give birth to change, he is the one to bring that baby to fruition. And....African Americans. Some of you may have thrown in the towel, wanted to give up, but God has thrown it back at ya. It's your time, the pain and adversity, have pushed you to use your voice. I hope this book gives others hope, & the inspired word to "Get on The Good Foot," Pull together a nation, a people of God, and unify this country. We have to unite by our similarities and not our differences to become again the great #1 country that we were once ranked. The world is waiting on us again, to rise up, and provide our leadership that they may find the trust & confidence to follow our lead again.

To All In the fight. My patients who struggle with mental illnesses & distress at all time high, African American, Latino, Asian brothers and sisters, all of those of other cultures who have experienced and continue to experience what it feels like to be caught up in the hands of injustice. An unequal playing field, where the scales are tipped against you. Those who believe in the prophetic. A timely word. A message to others of warning, direction or correction to bring about change. For others to make a change, this is for you! It can occur through verbal messages; a statement from a person(s), like, those experts in the sciences, Dr. Anthony Fauci, White House Coronavirus Task force used by God to Warn, Sound the Alarm of The Trends & wave of the Coronavirus. Rev. Al Sharpton, for his television program "Politics Nation" and his leadership/ voice to the African American community, & families, during the times of losses/grief, trouble and in the fight for social justice. Messages to people can be given in the form of preaching/or teachings, or as in this case moved by God to write & convey a message of HOPE of Change to Come to humanity.

—Rev. Dr. Lisa C. Townsend

CHAPTER 1

AMERICA WATCH YOUR STEP

What Past Missteps Have Taught Us.
A Look at History. What's in It for Me?
What's At Stake? Ever'y'thing!

For one, our slip is hanging, the countries achilles heel, weaknesses are being exposed.

The leader, the U.S., image is taking a blow. We have lost our footing and the country is surely coming off for all the world to see, shamefully & our footing awkwardly off balanced. At present the U.S. is no longer the #1 country in the world. To my shock, Canada was. According to a More recent report as of Jan. 2020 conducted by U.S. News, we have slipped down from our No.4 ranking, with Canada No.2 and Switzerland viewed as the world's No. 1 country. This is in part due to the current administration's policies, low assessment of the current president's character, growth in large gaps between the rich and poor, racial tensions, inequality. Also due to the sharpest drop in global trust since 2016 among all countries assessed, amongst other issues of concern. A look at history & what it has taught us is that, there are many missteps that we have made over the course of history as it pertains to racial inequality and injustice of African Americans, Slavery. Of course, we cannot also forget to mention the slavery of Native Americans. Before that the first enslaved Africans to set foot on the U. S. continental were brought by Spanish explorers with them - who revolted, then by the 1520's the indigenous people in the Spanish colony of Hispaniola were brought over and later died. Enslaved Africans were brought in to replace them in the search for gold. All which was the beginning of American's greed and little care for the poor or disenfranchised. Historically, our country was founded on these issues that justified slavery. It is catching up with us & continues to manifest itself, in the millennium, the turn of the 21st century, even in 2020. We haven't put these issues behind us.

QUESTIONS

1. After Reading the Intro of The Book, Where Were You & What Were You Doing When You Found Out About the Coronavirus (Covid-19)?

2. How Do You Think the U.S. Can Reconcile Their Differences with One Another, "Get on The Good Foot?

3. According to Readings in Chapter 1, Did You Know that America Slipped in Their Ranking as the #1 Country In The World?

4. The U.S. Was Always the World Leader, What Do You Think Caused Us to Fall from Our #1 Position in The World?

NOTES

NOTES

NOTES

_____

_____

_____

_____

_____

_____

_____

_____

_____

_____

_____

_____

CHAPTER 2

RELIGION'S FOOTHOLD, IMPACT ON SOCIAL-RACIAL INJUSTICE, & ROLE IN POLITICS?

Religion, Evangelicalism, Christianity have taken center stage during the last election and seems to be gaining a foothold in this election year. Conservative Christians-Evangelicalism is in the forefront our politics, now our supreme court vs. Progressive Christianity. However, this is not the first time. Historically, it was getting prayer out of schools, separation of church & state, and it won't be the last time that Christianity/or religion will be center stage in elections or social issues. What impact has it made on resolving the social issues America is currently facing? Such as racial injustice?

Religion-Christianity fails when it places other issues over the welfare/ equality of others. Or, one's politics over religion (To be Republican is to be Christian), or One's biblical sin over another biblical sin. How can it be beneficial? It can be when Evangelical Christians can separate the bible from their politics. Mindsets that places such value on issues of where a person stands on issues such as: pro-life vs. pro-choice, the legal term Roe vs. Wade when choosing a president, why is this the only issue Evangelical - Conservative Christians assess when determining a person's Godliness? or qualifications for president? Why don't Conservatives/Evangelicals care about racial justice and interfaith justice. When it comes to voting for a candidate they stress voting for the candidate that quotes scriptures, the person many of them say: Is on the right side of the bible, pro-choice. "Vote the issue, not the candidate."

Trump was considered on the right side of the bible because of Israel & his leadership of the events transpiring with the U.S. & Israel, moving the embassy & that move being a fulfillment of prophecy and what was projected to come, in the bible.

Voting the issue(s), was big on the Evangelical's list for those participating in the election. Meaning, for many conservatives, the few issues that mattered to them, the issues that they considered, during the 2020 election to line up closest to God, not the candidate. They don't always say: Trump, but there's an implied biase evidenced by pointing out of a few issues that his administration supported but exclusion of other issues that matter to God such as lying, divorce, oppressing the poor, suppression (as in voter suppression), freedom, murder, racism, prejudice, & mistreatment of children, which are lack of character.

To bring about change, one must begin questioning values that they have been taught around certain issues. Protecting the unborn is one issue, but what about a president not protecting children who are born & separated from their parents at the border? or again, character? As the bible states, we shall know them by the fruit they bear. Not what they say, but what they do. Both 2020 candidates, if you search hard enough, & some people you don't have to search hard at all, you will find flaws. The difference is their character. Their ability to show the fruits of love, patience, kindness, self-control. (KJVB Galatians 6:22) to admit error, apologize, Godly sorrow.

Satan, was one of the prettiest or beautiful fallen angels, maybe we could say he was a narcissist?, his sin was pride, he knew & knows the word of God, better than we humans. Read it it in

Genesis 3: 1-24, how he contributed to the fall of the first man and woman (Adam & Eve). For the sake of pages, let me resist the temptation here to PREACH!

What about the rich not paying their fair share of taxes they owe? Rendering to Caesar what is his? Helping the poor, the needy? The least of those amongst us?

For starters, continuing the mission of Jesus, which is to help end injustice to the poor, the widows, the orphans? Not to worship the false gods of wealth and power. All, which makes us greedy and little care for the poor. Yet, historically, the bible, religion, was used to justify slavery. All, a part of a system to maintain a belief or perception that a certain race of people, are better, supreme, privileged over others and a fight to maintain this status quo. A country that sees the world in black & white. We can learn something from our history. This has been the wrong foot to get off on and we need not try to go back there. We've got to Get on The Good Foot! America must switch its focus to the real enemy. Get on combat boots of Christianity, or what the bible calls the Christian's armor of footwear, is to have their feet shod (fitted) with the preparation of the gospel of peace (prepared to share God with all). People of God should put as much emphasis on the wrongfulness of slavery, inequality, injustice as it does for other sins and issues. God looks at all sin the same, equality and freedom for All men, not just a specific race of people. Where's one's moral compass? Once again, where is Religion's Impact on Social Justice?

The last time I read the book of Genesis 2:7 KJB translation. It states, "And the Lord God formed man of the dust of the ground, and breathed into his nostrils the breath of life, and man became a living being. I understand that he made All men and made them All out of the same elements, and equal. That is, indeed, the mind of Christ. It also hasn't helped with the leadership of the current administration; the president of the United States, perspective on the cause of social issues/ racial inequalities. Reflected in policies, and deflecting questions of systemic racism in regards to police brutality. it also doesn't help for evangelicals enabling this mindset, and not calling him out on inequality towards people of color. Moreover, as the law and order president, he encourages policemen to be tougher on people in violation of the law, taking actions beyond procedure. You could say history is repeating itself and It's reared its ugly head." Satan-Evil is in the midst. America continues to show its true colors.

The good news is that African Americans used religion to liberate themselves by embracing freedom of man in the bible and the rejecting of any mindset of supremacy of a race, and contrary to God's words in the bible. African Americans have been resilient but that does not mean there is no need for change in policies, help from other Christians, other Americans, advocacy, social, and criminal justice reform. Timeline of First African American Christians was before the civil war, 1788. They did & continue to do what they were made to think they could not do! An Eleanore Roosevelt quote says, "You Must Do the Thing You Think You Cannot Do." or I would add "Do The Thing that a society, a family, or other people have told you, you couldn't do." What that translates into is a faith. African Americans have always been people of strong faith in God. There are efforts through the Black church to combat voter suppression through education and souls to the polls. I participate in education through the local church, my counseling center, and work at the polls. Now that's Getting on The Good Foot.

As I said, the first Christians were before the civil war. Through my discussions with many Caucasians, they can't see the injustice that African Americans face because they have seen & see the strides/ advancement they have accomplished. My response in this much needed dialogue between different races of people, is that African Americans have made advancements, but they don't want undone all their hard work, that of the civil rights era, Dr. Martin Luther King, and other greats, to be reversed and go backwards.

The civil unrest of Black lives, which if they were not occurring, would not be a need for the Black Lives Matter Movement, which is not to say other lives don't matter, but the messaging is to bring the focus on the merciless losses of lives and to bring widespread attention to it, to do something about it. Change it. In the midst of this cancel culture were living in, activism and activist are needed more than ever. Its purpose is not to allow the African American man or woman's lives to be a victim of the cancel culture, canceled and made to be seen as without value like the value Caucasian & other races of people take pride in and the value that is shown them in society. But the greater point is…. racial divide is a distraction from resolving other issues such as health care, the economy, the pandemic, climate change, and moving forward not divided as red states & blue states, but the united states. The whole country should not want to go backwards on past issues & continue to repeat history. Something is trying to influence us to destroy one another.

Let's "Get on the Good Foot', Get to the real source of this countries issues and put a stop to it, together.

QUESTIONS

1. Do You Believe Religion Plays A Big Role in Helping to Solve Social Issues, Such As, Racism & Police Brutality-Deaths of African Americans? Historically, Looking Back, What Religions or Leaders Helped During Past Era's and A President's Administration? (Such as Civil Rights, etc.)

2. Do You Know of Any Televangelist, Pastors, Or Church Leaders Of Various Races, Who Speak Out Against Racism. Also, Deaths Of African Americans Caused by Police Brutality? What Should Religions Role Be in Politics When Issues of Division & Racism Play A Part of Problems in The Country? Should Electing Any American Candidate for Office, Especially, The Presidency Be A Factor? Or Should Religious Leaders, Only, Speak Out Against It, Or Both?

3. What Role Should Religion Play in Speaking Out Against Any Form(s) Of Prejudice? What Mindset(s) prevent You from Doing So? Any

Religious Denomination or Leader, That You Can Think Of?

4. Should Christians Be Biased Towards A Leader If They Don't Come From The Same Denomination as Themselves, Practice the Same Faith? Consider Them Not a Christian?

PRINCIPLES

Did You Know That as A Christian You Have the Obligation To Speak Out Against Any Injustices?

Also, There are No Sins That Are Worse Than Others? All Sins of a Leader, Or Any Person Should Be Made Clear That It Is Not Acceptable.

Set The Standard for The Moral Direction of Our Country. People Are Watching! When Christians Don't, It Adds to The Social Problems, It Turns Others Off and Affects Your Witness. After All, Your Witness Should Expand Beyond Those of Your Own Circle or Race.

Rev. Dr. Lisa C. Townsend

NOTES

_____

_____

_____

_____

_____

_____

_____

_____

_____

_____

_____

_____

NOTES

NOTES

_____

_____

_____

_____

_____

_____

_____

_____

_____

_____

_____

_____

CHAPTER 3

WHAT'S AT STAKE? WHAT DO WE HAVE TO LOSE?

To those of you reading this book, not much into religion, but just striving to be good people. Can I tell you; God is not of Division? He is a God of Addition, not Subtraction. He made us All diverse, to add to one another, for the good of us All. We're stronger together, than apart. This is the change that has to be accepted and embraced. That's right, We All, Everyone. Or, rather the weak, gullible, uneducated, and I don't mean formal education, will have to be aware that at the end of this deception, if we don't Get On the Good Foot, head in the opposite direction, turn these problems around, and embrace change, we'll continue to keep our eyes on the wrong issues, off of our real enemy and it will result in All of us being destroyed. We are, I must say again, America, is certainly coming off looking sloppily, with unorthodox footing, off balance and our slip is hanging as other countries look on as we are pitted against our own country men, divided in our own country, one race against another. "United We Stand, Divided, We Fall."

We definitely can't have the same respect that other countries had for us with this divisive display.

The handling of the Coronavirus sealed the unfavorable view of the U.S, which is as low as it has ever been according to the pew report which began polling nearly two decades ago. We, (as in All of us who are U.S. citizens) lose the respect, fairness & dignity of former 3 Presidents Barack Obama, Bill Clinton, George W. Bush, etc. once brought to the country irregardless of party differences & policies. It's been reported in various news outlets, that the power of police unions and the racism of the U.S. congress under all the above mentioned presidents, including Donald Trump, both democrats and republicans, police violence had grown worse. The difference, Donald Trump provided the Kerosene. He prided himself on being the law & order president, but turned the oval office into the place where he incited racial, ethnic, and cultural division. Not only was he racist, but sexist, misogynistic, homophobic, and every other "ist" and "ic."

Rev. Dr. Lisa C. Townsend

Historically, January 1, 1863 President Lincoln issued The Emancipation Proclamation, which came about by an executive order, freeing the slaves. January 11, 1944 Franklin D. Roosevelt; signed a bill known as the "Second Bill of Rights", The economic bill of rights for unemployment insurance, food, clothing, and shelter. On July 2, 1964, Southern politician, President Lyndon B. Johnson signed into law the Bipartisan Civil rights Act of 1964, which prohibited discrimination in public places, provided for the integration of public schools, facilities, and made employment discrimination based on race illegal. Prior to that, less than two months Rev. Dr. Martin Luther King gave the Historical "I have a Dream" speech at the Lincoln Memorial. It would seem, President Johnson, recognized the importance of uniting the country and the only way to be effective in his presidency meant creating equality for All people, & the only way to unite the country.

What we learned historically from these past presidencies is that they were leading into the pressures that the country called for, which produces great social justice. But it, also bridges the gap in the country, unites,and brings about social justice. There wasn't a blatant disregard for the fact that there is certainly more that

37

unites us, than divides us. They were certainly looking out for, historically their legacy & mark on the country. These presidents could not have successful presidencies without policies to benefit all. They had to influence all people,get them working together and uniting for the common good. As the census is being taken and reported, Latinos continue to grow in numbers, becoming the largest race in the U.S. With this being a fact and what history has taught us, a good leader, on right footing & in the right mind knows to be most effective, powerful, you have to win the influence & have the leadership ability to unite all people that you have to reside over for a common good and successful execution of a specific goal. Only one who fears that they cannot do so, will lead by divisive measures & division, hook or crook.

We ALL as a country have everything to lose. Our democracy, economy, and standing in the world. At, present, according to Policy Magazine's, latest ranking in Oct 2020, the U.S. ranked 33 out of 36 countries in foreign policy on how well the Coronavirus outbreak was handled. Turkey, Russia, and Iran are behind the U.S. Russia, for the recorded cases daily and Iran for recorded deaths daily. As we weaken, and show cracks in our countries armor, our National Security is also at risk. Is it worth it?! There is more that ALL of the people in the U.S. have in common for the common good of All of us.

Absolutely, there is more that unites us, than divides us! Other countries are beginning to place travel bans on U.S. citizens. Doesn't matter the color of your skin. Your race. Americans were always welcomed, admired, looked up to. It's time to "Get On The Good Foot!" To avoid starting off on the wrong foot as the country moves forward. We must start on the right foot, or to correct or restart on the right footing, & with the proper Stance/ Stand, America! If we don't Stand against injustices, discrimination and inequality, we will fall for anything. Don't fall for the lies of fear, …We must turn this country around, determine the direction we are headed in, if it is not for the good of All, then turn and head in the opposite direction. If we continue to do the same thing we have previously done; we will continue to get the same results. We got a bad addiction, the drug is inequality, and the high is power. Supremacy. We have got to "Get on The Good Foot, Pronto!

QUESTIONS

1. Was This Chapter an Eye Opener/Did It Open Your Eyes to Some New Information? Did It Change How You Looked at Our Country As A Whole?

2. Was There a Shift You Experienced from an "Us" Vs. "Them" Mindset To "We?"

3. What's in It for You? What's at Stake for The Whole Country?

PRINCIPLES

A Good Leader, Especially, The President of The United States, Can Not Have A Successful Administration, Or Legacy By Leading The Country or Any Other Organization, Or Business by Division. They Have to Unite All People for A Common Purpose. It May Last For A Season, But They Will Soon Find That They Are Standing on A Shaky Footing When Their Empire Falls.

NOTES

_____

_____

_____

_____

_____

_____

_____

_____

_____

_____

_____

NOTES

_____

_____

_____

_____

_____

_____

_____

_____

_____

_____

_____

NOTES

_____

_____

_____

_____

_____

_____

_____

_____

_____

_____

_____

CHAPTER 4

GOOD FOOTING & MENTAL FITNESS

Lessons from Most Effective Sports, Athletics, And Building Principles

So, we now know where we first heard this saying; "Get on The Good Foot," in the James Brown funk song "Get on the Good Foot." released in 1972, energizing & urging people to get started right. Do it right, with power. But, more importantly we can learn from athletes and builders how poor footing in performance or a structure can can sabotage good results, but it can be turned around with correction, Good Footing & proper stance. We, are being urged based on the state of the United States Of America to begin again and Get it right. This country has lost its footing, gotten off on the wrong foot, a shaky start & poor foundation, resulting in loss of power.

The negative effects, state of affairs in the U.S. in

regard to racial injustice, has been since slavery, the 17th century, 1619. That is why I have said that we, as a country started off on the wrong foot and got off to a bad start! We're starting to forget what it means to be an American. Built by the hands of Black slaves, immigrants, ... We are all feeling the tension, pressure, like never before. Just as a builder preparing a structure. They know the importance of proper footing & placement. A support when creating a firm foundation, to obtain balanced pressure on the footing. That is why we are all feeling the tension, pressure like never before because we don't have proper footing & the power/pressure of support is imbalanced, causing the U.S. to be virtually, off balanced as a country.

In addition to this, to have good balance, one must have sound concentration and mental sharpness. One must not be distracted, but keep its mind focused on the proper target. That includes critical thinking, learning & using good judgement. Athletes. Tennis players know the importance of being in a good mind & that proper footing (Your anchor) helps one to have good balance & power when hitting the ball and aim for the right shot. Football, the sport my Uncle Nathaniel Herron excelled in is noted as the best sport to grasp proper footing. Good Footwork effects agility, ability to "Get on The Good Foot," move one's feet quickly. Fast feet can help a football player sprint, change direction, block and tackle. Boxing, which is a professional sport I have worked in and a family of professional and amateur boxing champions, including my father & hall of famers. Good footing allows a Boxer to hit harder, get out of danger and puts one in proper position to hit target. There are multiple ways to stand, but you cannot box or fight your opponent well without getting your stance right. For those of you more familiar with tennis, Martial Arts, which I ministered & made reference to in a Sunday sermon "Spiritual Judo," Fighting God's way, the same proper footing rules apply. This country is in a fight on war.

As I previously stated, Former Vice President to Barack Obama, Joe Biden has said during his run for 2020 presidency, "We are fighting for the soul of Nation." We are the United States, not the divided States. So, you may be asking yourself as you read this chapter, so... Dr Lisa, what can we learn from this? That there is a way that we have to fight to win & getting on proper footing means playing by the proper, unspoken rule. Which is, ...We not a singular race of people, are a group of many races and the way to fight is to unite. We may be opponents, at times, we are not one another's enemy. We are a melting pot, built by the hands of black slaves, diversity of cultures, immigrants, etc... We must make sure were positioned to hit the right target, leaning on All of our fellow Americans as supports, to hold the structure, not target practice for those we have to live amongst, labor & fight for our country with.

Rev. Dr. Lisa C. Townsend

QUESTIONS

1. Is Division Amongst Those One Has to Live with In This Country An Enemy to One's Critical Thinking, Such as One's Focus And Ability To "Get on The Good Foot," Focus on The Real Enemy, & Task At Hand?

2. Do You Count the Cost? Does the Negative Effects of Getting Off On the Wrong Foot of Division, Outweigh the Good That We Could Be Experiencing in The U.S.?

3. As A Bridge Builder, Do You See Your Fellow Country Men & Women as Supports to Lean On, Take the Weight Off of One Another, And Keeping the Country on A Solid Foundation?

4. How Can One Apply the Principles in Chapter 4, Of Seeing Others as Supports Like A Builder, Or as An Athlete, Exercising Critical Thinking & Maintaining Good Footing by Not Being Distracted by Ones Differences, In One's Own Family?

49

5. Can You Think About the Question Above; In Terms of Solving Problems, Not Being Distracted by The Wrong Issues?

6. Do You Think About Enlisting Others with Different Opinions, Of Various Cultures & Races to Unite With To Help You Problem Solve?

PRINCIPLE

Remember,…A House Divided by Itself Cannot Stand! Matthew 12:22-28 KJVB

Abraham Lincoln

NOTES

_____

_____

_____

_____

_____

_____

_____

_____

_____

_____

_____

NOTES

_____

_____

_____

_____

_____

_____

_____

_____

_____

_____

_____

NOTES

_____

_____

_____

_____

_____

_____

_____

_____

_____

_____

_____

_____

CHAPTER 5

AMERICA'S GOT A BAD CASE OF ATHLETES FOOT!

THE DISEASE & THE CURE

Disease is what a doctor diagnoses, something mankind has and needs to be cured of. As simple as I tried to make it, America has to go further than tell people what the issues of the country are, as if it can be just nipped in the bud. No more than I can just tell them through this book that we need to "Get on the Good Foot," change, Pronto. We can't just educate what's at risk & what the country has to lose, and pump up individuals to make decisions from a moral compass, or the urgency to change, or a catchy phrase, to energize one. We can wage a good war, a direct attack on the disease, educate, let others know what's at stake for the country as a whole, to try to keep it under control.

However, like a disease we have no cure or vaccine for, we've been trying to treat the symptoms/

sicknesses of fear, racism, power, superiority, greed, etc… But, without focusing on a cure for the disease. We try to treat the symptoms, keep it under control but under certain conditions signs of disease, over time, continue to show a long history of being gone unchanged year after year. Over the last 4 years division has increased in the U.S. The reason the country has not been able to "Get On the Good Foot" & unite, be a melting pot, is because when individuals make decisions, or vote during presidential elections such as the 2020 election. It was based on their conditions, not a moral compass. The country has been split. Trump voters estimated at some 70 million. The other remaining votes for Joe Biden. Half vote the issues, others vote their condition.

There is another margin, who vote the welfare of the country such as; if people were wealthy, many voted for the candidate who was against raising their taxes, not the one to change the system, as this could change their conditions. The fear is change & the impact that it may have on maintaining the status quo. The state of affairs of some is not the same for others. That causes the divide. It appeared that half of people were looking at how each candidate & the plan towards policy and other changes would adversely affect their hard- earned incomes, and quality of one's own life. It's better for some than others. We have to bridge the gap between these disparities. Rest assured, Yes, there are exceptions. The disease of division has permeated our country and plagued it throughout history. Equality is the cure.

There is an equality divide and we have to create a level playing field, bridge the gap between the two Americas, making equal opportunity for everyone. We have to begin to shift the values of the people in our country by using positive reinforcement and reward giving and caring for others, not just having money/riches.

America has a disease. In a nutshell, Americas got a bad case of Athletes Foot. That I will use for sake of my point, as a metaphor. An infection caused by organisms. They can be helpful or hurtful, but under certain conditions some organisms may cause disease. America, just can't "Get on The Good Foot!" We need something to attack the illness or organism(s) contributing to the disease & cure it, not just treat it. Athletes foot is catchy, contagious. it spreads. In that way just as the Coronavirus. Not as severe or deadly, but with certain events and contact. Individuals can be given treatment such as medicine to help it, but it is not cured, because they still have the condition. Some people just aren't able to be cured. They were treated, but the condition of the virus, remained.

For Clarity. The illness/or sickness /symptom(s) is Fear, the disease is Division. The sickness is an abnormal seeking of power/control in an area of lack or something that one feels an inferiority about and seeks to acquire through things or people, to compensate for this deficit. Once they acquire something to fill the void, there's a fear of losing it.

So.ooo, individuals project superiority onto others as if those people are inferior to them. They use systemic racism and unjust means to do so, but the problem is theirs. The illness is fear (of their inferiority, the need to prove their better, different, not equal), but the disease is division. This is what got the country off on wrong footing. "Some people try to be tall by cutting off the heads of others" —Paramahansa Yogananda.

Alfred Adler, Theory of Inferiority Complex suggested that every person has a sense of inferiority. But it is those that act on it that cause divisiveness. Adler adds, from childhood, people work towards overcoming this inferiority by striving for superiority. But it is the need to prove this by the abuse of power & others, and behaviors which leads us to Police brutality, voter suppression- pandemics, murders-losses of lives. The millions of deaths as a result of COVID-19 stems from President Trump's overestimation of his superiority and under estimation of the virus. Police brutality/injustice resulted in 21 deaths alone this year 2020, of African Americans at the time of this book, Because it was perceived as something that affects the lower class, "Those people," the one's with something inherently wrong with them.

Let me recap, for the sake of this chapter, the trauma/disease that many of us have had to endure in 2020. At the time this book went to production, black lives matter protest of George Floyd, his words to police "I can't breathe, which became a Black Lives Matter protest slogan and the words he uttered before his death. The loss of Breonna Taylor, & many more. 2014 to 2019, deaths of African Americans that were disproportionately by police resulted in 6,557 deaths in the united states. In addition to rise in deaths by police, there was rise in mental health with more than a 1,000 percent increase in

April 2020 from reports the same time last year. Deaths, grief/loss, fires, floods, racial tensions and divisions turned up!!!! Just a distraction. When ordinary people take note of these issues, injustices, get involved, & act, the playing field becomes leveled. You can hold leaders in high office, accountable! All people can pull up economically, from lower economic stature, and raise up on the hierarchy in the American class system. (Chapter 7 details interventions).

So...., after reading this again were you able to empathize with the struggle of those I mentioned? Do You believe that America needs To Get On The Good Foot and cure this disease, which may take compromise on All Americans behalf? or were you not able to relate to the plight of these individuals, or race of people because it is not your current condition? Equality, the cure, will change this inability to sympathize or emphathize with others, and bring unity.

QUESTIONS

1. Do You Agree That U.S. Has A Disease & It's Time To Stop Just Treating It Because We Have the Cure & We All Just Need to Do Our Part by Letting Go of Mindsets Of Superiority?

2. Do You Believe That Other Contributions to Our Country Should Be Shown Value (Rewarded), Not Just Having Money/Being Rich to Help Create Equality?

3. Do You Have an Us & Them Mindset/ Thinking?

4. If You Stated, Yes, To the Question Above....... How Will That Make A Good Leader, Or A Politician Who Can Govern All People, & Make the Country Better for All?

5. How Does Superiority/Supremacy Mindsets Perpetuate the Cycle, Cause Problems for Your Children & Family? Also, Continue to Perpetuate The Cycle of Spreading Fungus & Disease in The Country?

Rev. Dr. Lisa C. Townsend

NOTES

_____

_____

_____

_____

_____

_____

_____

_____

_____

_____

_____

NOTES

_____

_____

_____

_____

_____

_____

_____

_____

_____

_____

_____

NOTES

_____

_____

_____

_____

_____

_____

_____

_____

_____

_____

_____

CHAPTER 6

THE "GOOD" FOOT, "BAD", & THE "UGLY":

My Personal Experience

I've been fortunate to experience the good side of justice and the bad side of injustice/Inequality. Because of that, I can not only sympathize with others pain, but I can also empathize with them.

One, experience was professional and one personal. I could not wait to see President Trumps presidency come to an end. I had never seen such systemic racism, oppression, attack on one's person, social workers, psychologist, and human services worker's like myself, ever in my life, or in any other administration.

I've experienced African Americans have to fight for themselves, while trying to care and do the right thing for their patients. This can be expensive, costly. Advocating for clients and being objective can bring licensed professionals under great burden and scrutiny if one were to buck the system.

One can be under a microscope and get in some deep trouble. In the last 4 years, caring & looking out for the best interest of clients is secondary. Money was primary. Insurmountable co-pays. If were not for Obama Care, patients, no matter how dire the needs, would not have been able to be seen. It's not about what professionals did to help individuals, but what could be found that one did not do, to resist approving change. There's a lot of fault finding & projection to prevent professionals from taking action that may change or upset the status quo. Trying to go above and beyond to help the poor, people of color, those tied to the system, same race clients, history of mental illness, family dysfunction, and oppression can place a target on an African American licensed, professionals back. Many are being shorted in pay for services and time rendered. It is often times not worth fighting because of the legalities and scrutiny that one would be placed under, being licensed. Many court cases arise out of conflicts regarding pay. People/ or a system, taking advantage, using the system, and looking for a way out of paying. There are also people being hired in similar job descriptions and duties without the licensing, education, experience or burden.

I know this to also, be true for other races of people also, who enter their professions to help and bring about change and find themselves outsiders, lacking the resources, and connections to those who are part of the status quo to protect themselves, while reaching others.

Much of mental health has been about money making for many insurance companies & systems, off of those programs or individuals tied to them. Joe Biden also mentioned in one of his speeches that his daughter was a social worker and was payed very low for her hard work, education and experience. It can be a fight and tiring as an outsider.

The second experience I faced from 2016-2020, was personal. It increased during COVID-19, 2020. I have experienced problems in my neighborhood in the suburbs where I have had to phone the police & they were objective and fair. It wasn't the police, but the neighbors. For the information of those who believe the myth that African Americans don't live in the suburbs. They are there, and have been for years. My family have lived in the suburbs for over 30 years and when we arrived there, they were not Caucasian women, who were stay at home moms and did not work. If they were not working out of the home; they were working, babysitting, or some work to bring extra needed money into the household. To live in the neighborhood, they weren't college educated or with high paying jobs. They were hard working, hustlers. Doing various jobs to earn money & support their family. Many, of the women were the bread winners.

Most of the time, the men were out of work and the women carried the family. It reminded me of hardworking African American and other races of women, who are highly educated with college degrees over males. I never saw color, until racist actions were displayed and those observations only showed me that there was not much differences in those people who lived in the suburbs, I lived amongst. The difference in it, the suburbs that is...,vs. the inner city, is the people's old mindsets and system. I had to learn quickly the climate. People kept their lawns well cut, just as my family had always done. But, behind that exterior were people who were financially hurting like other races of people. They were having their lights, gas, etc. shut off.

Presidential candidate Joe Biden is an individual

who can identify with this. I'm sure what I have shared is not new to him. He is diversified by his knowledge of different races of people, especially the African American community, his adversities, and plans unite us. He has been an example of being realistic, reality- based, about the world we are now living in, and truth about the people who are the makeup of the United States of America. Wake up people! "Get on The Good Foot" and choose a president who will lead you by being honest with you about reality. He displays empathy, cultural awareness and sensitivity.

Here's the cure. This will heal you of the sickness of anger and rage stemming from racist attitudes, frustration, hateful behavior and cure you of the disease it creates, "Division." They also eat at you from inside. These outward manifestations/ symptoms, haven't stopped, and won't stop this country and other races of people from continuing to move forward. This is not an endorsement of Biden, but a vision of change, with someone with one foot squarely planted on the ground to turn this country in a different direction and propel it forward. Biden can be the president of All Americans. He knows the injuries of Black, White, All of Americans.

He can't solve every issue and won't be able to, but he is the one to lead us, the way forward. This country will be able to "Get on the Good Foot", by not just treating the symptoms of its disease and putting a bandaide on them, but cure it. America will then be able obtain good footing to bring solidarity back to this country. I know this is being very ambitious of me. But the vision is of not seeing increased signs of the disease, but a decrease, to almost none at all.

It was confirmed to me in the suburbs that White Americans (Caucasian) are hurting and have issues of being left behind and out. Also, it is worth reminding, that they aren't all rich, just because they are "White' and they don't all come from functional families, or don't have issues like other races. They fear this exposure. Those perceptions diminish the hardships of White Americans in the minds of other races. Many Caucasians fear losing that superior mental foothold, but it also prevents others from identifying with their pain and struggles.

That may be the reason many whites have trouble with the "Black lives Matter" slogan & movement. It's in the interpretation. Because, as some of my patients have conveyed to me, they are thinking about /of the oppression of many of them. They can reflect on pain their families have experienced and their lack. They have been rejected/rejects. But Black Lives Matter is in response to the deaths & senseless murders that black people & their families have suffered at the hands of police brutality. It is in disproportionate numbers to other races. Not that Caucasian's lives or any other race of people's lives doesn't matter. The time that blacks receive for crimes & incarceration are insurmountable to whites. Despite, "White Privilege." it doesn't apply to all. All African Americans are not convinced that they are inferior, and their lives have no value. It is a systemic problem. But it is projected by society, as if it is because blacks are bad, cursed or as the Reverend Al Sharpton has stated, "Inherently inferior." When low income is spoken of in the news, it is assumed by many that it is African Americans, Latinos, etc....

I stated above, I've seen my Caucasian brothers & sisters in suburban neighborhoods have gas & lights shut off because of financial struggles. If they are in violation of parking or other violations, and reported to the police, if the police come out to their home, they will be home, but will not answer the door. The front, side, back or any other. On contrast, African Americans in neighborhoods feel that it is the right thing to do, to answer if a police officer comes to their home & knocks on the door. I would also say; that we fear not answering the door to find out what they want, but also the thought that there may be some negative ramifications such as; adding to mistrust or suspicion and contributing to them looking through windows, to kick the door in, shoot, etc. They just know how to cover, the biblical saying, "sowing on fig leaves. in reference to Adam & Eve, in the Garden of Eden, covering up their nakedness & sin, flaws, inadequacies, from being exposed (after all, their just like everyone else; even black & brown and other races of people), by taking fig leaves from the trees, they were attempting to cover their nakedness (sin). Prevent it from being exposed (Genesis 3: 7 KJBV. Read it). By continuing to keep the lawn mowed and the white picket fences, and maintain all the adornments & flowers. An image of pure, perfect.

Just Like, the CoVid Virus. Hardship comes on all. Even, whites, who aren't upper middle class or the wealthy. It doesn't discriminate based on color, creed, age, gender, rich or poor. Like a (Caucasian) city worker said to me when he was making an observation in a neighborhood and witnessed an individual being judgmental, exclaimed; "That's why you don't go throwing stones at glass houses".

That metaphor "Gave Me My Life", as I would say in slang. Hope! We were finding common ground. Able to be real about America. Because of false perceptions, there will always be some who don't want people of color there, in suburbia. But, the truth is they are there and have been. In suburbia, racist individuals know how to use the city ordinances, the system, to complain and harass those they don't want there. To display their sense of superiority & power. Cover up for feeling inferior to, not measuring up to the people of color living amongst them. Even, when they were living there before them. That's a sad state to me. As a Christian/ Minister, I have to remember to also not let these experiences affect my witness for God as well, although challenging, to say the least.

Police were a help to me in ensuring that conflicts didn't rise out of control, to not fall into any traps to set me up to compromise my integrity in being provoked to behave in a way that would put my professional career in jeopardy. They were well trained and appeared unbiased. For this, I am grateful! I can truly say that All police aren't bad.

On the other hand, I want to add, having had to be a whistle blower at one point in my career, whistle blowers don't fare well during this time, 2016-2020, current administration. I'm believing a change in leadership will bring integrity back to the country and measures are taken to clean up cover up & corruption from Washington, down to the mainstream America. I firmly believe the fungus from leadership, spreads from the top down. Change & being a Christian, pointing individuals to Jesus Christ, not a man, or an issue(s), where they are able to get free of a system, and use their religious beliefs to choose for themselves and become independent of the system will put a target on your back. It, change that is, will not be embraced and will be viewed as something to be feared if it is different, changes mindsets & perceptions, or a challenge to individuals maintaining the status quo. Advocacy/Activism is the cornerstone upon which social work is built. It is so important that it is framed in three sections of The Code of Ethics: Advocacy for individuals, communities and systems. It is not a choice; it is a prerequisite. (NASW).

Yes, getting on the Good Foot, means being wise & cautious, but it does not mean for us to be paralyzed & do nothing for fear of repercussions. Police officers need to have their cameras on them & turned on and policies should support that. Professionals like myself need to not only have their documentation, because when you're dealing with injustice that can be left to the systems own interpretation, so you need witnesses, and if possible, bring the case to the forefront of the public through the media if you want any chance of the real issues being exposed and to bring about change. As exhausting as that can be…., this is the state that we are living in during these times, systemic racism, as well as injustice for black,brown, & other cultures of people. We've got to get back on good footing. I can't help but cringe, thinking of the good policemen who can get into some life threatening or complicated situations trying to protect others and not take the risk to do so because of repercussions.

I reference the spiritual for this book because I believe that everything is indicative of a spiritual issue and need for healing. It is time for America to Get on Good footing & begin to turn from their former & present ways of treating All humanity. 2 Chronicles 7:14; If my people who are called by my name will humble themselves, and pray, seek my face and turn from their wicked ways, then shall they hear from heaven, and I will heal their land. That, even means Christians. They have to have accountability and that may mean associating & studying, dialoging about the bible with other people who don't look, sound, or come from the same place they come from.

Many of us are shaped by our environments and experiences & we can receive transference from trauma & pain we have experienced at the hands of others, which can bias our opinion of certain races or gender of people.

STAND UP FOR WHAT'S RIGHT, TAKE ACTION. GET INTO SOME Good Trouble!

Do the courageous thang, do the right thing (for millenniums - a reference from a Spike Lee Movie) stand up for the right thang, even thou it would land you on the bad side of the powers that be, Stand Up! Get into some trouble that's bad, but Good. Martin Luther King and many others got into bad situations: beaten, jailed. Bad, but it was for the good. The bible refers to proper footing/footwear as Christians. To be equipped. It is one of the seven pieces of armor discussed in my book The Christian Counselor Trend Handbook:

Will the Real Christian Counselors Stand Up?! Putting on The Whole Armour of God. Ready, equipped to bring Good News, who announce peace, the good news of happiness, etc. What is it that the apostle Paul notes that we do with the feet, our footing, that we do with no other part of our body? We Walk. We walk, the walk, not just talk, the talk. Take specific steps in bringing about peace & good for the lives of others, all humanity. Country, it's time to get on the good foot. If we, the USA don't get this together, we will destroy each other and our democracy. After all, "A House Divided Cannot Stand." (Matthew 12:22-28 KJVB,), United we stand, divided we fall. Again, there is more that unites us, than divides us. To make change, we All can be instrumental on small levels.

QUESTIONS

1. Do You Have Some Good/ Bad Experiences with Injustice?

2. How Can You Get Yourself into Some Good-Necessary Trouble, As Civil Rights Leader, U.S. Rep., Congressman John Lewis, Urged Us?

3. Are You Aware That You Have Mindsets That Breed Hateful & Other Issues, Behavior(s) That Will Eat at You from Within? Do You Question Them? Ask Yourself Where They Come From? Who Are You Accountable to? Holds You Accountable?

4. Do You Know That Mindsets as Mentioned in The Question Above Can Start Eating at You from Inside? But Manifest Outside, In Mental Illness(es) & Physical Health Illness(es), And Disease(s)?

*One can Also Seek the Help of a Therapist or Program in Their Community.

NOTES

NOTES

_____

_____

_____

_____

_____

_____

_____

_____

_____

_____

_____

NOTES

_____

_____

_____

_____

_____

_____

_____

_____

_____

_____

CHAPTER 7

LEVELS OF ADVOCACY & STEPS TO BRING ABOUT CHANGE

How the Average Individual Can Make Change on A Micro- Local & Community Macro, and Mezzo Level?

I. Micro-Level Practice

The most common type of change human services workers, therapist, and psychologist can utilize is one of the the social workers 3 levels of practice. Its focus is on, assessing and addressing an Individual's problems through one-on-one or small group assessments and treatment. It is called micro level practice when helping clients creatively solve problems, help people find housing, health care and social services, through gov't, state, or local authorized programs and interventions. It is this type skill of practice that makes communities safer with advocacy groups, lobbying activities, etc. They can be found in think tanks, advocacy groups, government agencies, and nonprofit groups. Helping a child in foster care, locating housing for a homeless person, family therapy and individual counseling. Therapists are not just in a clinical setting, behind a nice desk, and couch counseling an individual client or family. And… this is where the average individual person's skills come in to view, for those who want to make societal change.

You look around in your neighborhoods, your community, and do not like what you see or hear. The disparities, prejudice, inequality in housing, policing, neighborhood disputes, property values, etc. You wonder what you can do? You're not a therapist, counselor, or social worker, or maybe you do not work in the human services field. You don't have to sit idly by, reach out to help an individual solve a problem, have one-on-one dialogue or interaction with a person who you know & are respected by, who may have prejudices, lack resources, or knowledge of laws or ordinances, or actions that one may be oblivious to, which add to continued disputes between others or neighbors.

One should not enable the individual, neither do they need to mediate or get in the middle of the conflict between others, or take sides, on a micro level. An Example of this, is a retired neighbor of mine. He would visit, spend time one-on-one with individuals and have conversations with them. He didn't like for person to describe an individual by their race, such as the white family, black, Asian etc. or any other nationality. He preferred that you identify the person by their name, house they lived in, or some other description. He also didn't gossip provide negative feedback about a neighbor or provide any info about that person, disputes with others, or any of their character flaws, that would add fuel to the fire. It worked, because he showed that form of communication or discussion about other races of people was not the norm, or standard.

One can implement small actions like the ones mentioned above or other measures on a local level to come against and speak out on injustices such as: Make anonymous calls to your local authorities, protest, or if that is not your method of choice, lobby with organizations, in your local, state, and community.

There are many opportunities in Washington D.C. to also get involved in marches, connect with a diverse group of individuals, and educational opportunities. You can learn more about democracy and policies that affect change for marginalized groups of people. This knowledge can be brought back to one's community leaders, local, as well as, state officials, or on a micro level just individuals you live amongst.

II. Macro Level Change Efforts

Policy, program development for small and large communities, advocacy. Example: Black Lives Matter is a political & social movement advocating for non-violent civil disobedience in protest against incidents of police brutality and all racially motivated violence against black people. This is an effort that doesn't require one to be a human services professional or have a college education. You can also do the same thing within your own local Community to impact it. Also, efforts on a State, or National level can be taken for a cause close to one's heart and one is passionate about.

III. Mezzo Level

Professionals are involved in facilitating treatment groups. development and implementation of social service initiatives at the local and small community, Intermediate levels. They serve on the staff of schools, hospitals, community centers. Doesn't focus on individual, widespread community needs. Individuals can volunteer and assist in these efforts.

- Change on A Religious Level - (I added for the sake of this book):

- Get active, start or express interest in a "souls to the polls" at one's local church, or encourage others to come out to participate in the event.

- Develop programs to assist the disenfranchised or work with a group to do so.

- Churches can collaborate with leaders in one's community.

- Be active in neighborhoods

- Advance communications, technologies, and science.

- Involvement with the local police dept., court systems, schools, Jails, prisons, agencies/or organizations

- Practice activism. Organize marches during injustice, or inequality.

All of the afore mentioned; The average person can volunteer and assist professionals in doing.

Prayer - For one's neighborhood, community,

and state. One can broaden that effort and pray for their country and gov't. This can be done individually as I emphasize small efforts the individual person can exercise & it doesn't take participation in a group, or need be lengthy, or take much time. Although one can pray with others, as well, to come into agreement. There is power in numbers.

QUESTIONS

1. According to Chapter 7, How Can You, Without Being A Human Services Professional, Make Change on A Micro, Mezzo, And Macro Level?

2. Can You See the Need of Understanding Change from The Macro, Mezzo, & Micro Framework for Social Work and How It Affects Change?

3. How Will the Model in Chapter 7, It Effect Your Choice of Efforts To Get Involved In, Change the World, But Also Impact on Your Family? How Could It Influence Which Issues One Will Vote On, or Support?

4. If You Are a Professional, How Will This Model Help You to Reassess Your Efforts & Reprioritize Advocacy Based on Most Important Issues Affecting Your Patients or Clients?

NOTES

_____

_____

_____

_____

_____

_____

_____

_____

_____

_____

NOTES

_____

_____

_____

_____

_____

_____

_____

_____

_____

_____

_____

NOTES

_____

_____

_____

_____

_____

_____

_____

_____

_____

_____

_____

CHAPTER 8

CLOSING

"We" Won! Foot Gear. Losing The Battle, Winning The War.

A Dose of Optimism. Forward

I am optimistic that change can occur. How about you? African American people, in 2020, have experienced major setbacks in the criminal justice system, health disparities and comebacks. Mountain tops and valleys. A Faith in God. That's the only way, they as a people, individuals & their families have been able to make it. They have their errors, weak points, and some fall away from their source which is their spirituality & obedience to God. Liken, to other cultures of people, God has always been with them. When, We, Americans, ban together, it has always changed our course of direction for our country, during a crisis. We did it before and we can do it again. One nation under

God, indivisible, with liberty, & justice for All. We did it during…The Great Depression-1933,1940 -The preparation for the World War, by 1945 - bringing the U.S. on the verge of victory over all of its enemies. 1968- Richard Nixon's promise to decrease violence at home, bring the country together, and end the Vietnam war. The similarities each era shared was a common purpose for the country and a legacy of achievement that each president could be defined by in unifying a people. At the hem of it, African Americans! The country succeeded; it was a collaborative effort & leadership recognizing that. To defeat the Coronavirus, it takes all of us social distancing, wearing mask & not just African Americans, Asians, or Latinos, etc…The virus does not discriminate, it is an equal opportunity adversary. It doesn't matter your age, income bracket, or color of your skin. When we are exposed to the virus, we need the assistance from All essential workers, irregardless of their race.

America is finding its footing. We have demonstrated the ability to take on a collaborative effort. It takes this collaborative effort to come out of a crisis and solve a problem. I believe God can speak through an audible voice, the bible, or through circumstances. Are you hearing

him? Whenever, America has gotten off track
& on the wrong footing, historically, we've gone
through crisis to direct us back to our strength to
solve the problem, and that has been our ability
to come to together collectively. We"ve had to
reset! At the close of the 2020 election, that is
what had begun to take place.

African Americans lost many lives at the fault of
a broken criminal justice system. They suffered
what appeared to be defeats, but they didn't allow
the fear to stop them, instead, it pushed them to
capitalize on some fatal missteps. At their hands,
along with others, African Americans, Hispanic
Americans, Native Americans, Caucasian Americans,
etc., got this country off on" The Good Foot!" We
RESET. Reversed & turned the direction of the
country around. The people declared that we
would Do It Again, this time differently. Like
resetting a bone in a broken foot. The people
set the course to heal a broken nation along with
a Presidential Nominee who committed to unite
America. It not an endorsement of republican
or democrat…but, more important, Democracy
and the voice of the people was heard, their
decision was acted upon.

The time this book went to production, I am
elated to write that Joseph Robinette Biden Jr.

was elected the 46th President of the United States of America. Kamala Harris has become the first African American and Asian American, female Vice President, with Native American and Jamaican ancestry. Many of the divisions exasperated by the former president created a national nightmare. But, the people have spoken. They are ready to start the year on a new foot. They will "Get on The Good Foot." We're back to winning. Away with Native Americanism, xenophobism, racism, isolationism, the darkest part of populism. They have an eb & flow. We must take heed and not become slack. Stay woke and active in paying attention to our system, the policies, and continue to vote in full force to determine who sits in that oval office, occupies the Presidency... Because, if WE don't, those "isms" could flow again, anytime. America has spoken! We want to build bridges, not walls. We've fought some los-ing battles, but now, well on our way to winn-ing the war!

Forward

"He Picked Me Up, Turned Me Around, And Placed My Foot on A Solid Ground."

Special thanks to my mom and partner in business, Mary Herron Townsend. Because of you, we are a female, Mother-Daughter, Black-owned, business who serves multi-cultural populations, and our passion for diversity. To All The various ethnicities and cultures of volunteers, interns, and collaborations with churches. Project Reach Services Christian Counseling & Personal Growth Center, you are my baby from God, nurtured from the ground up, who told Me to "REACH My People!", "I will equip you, give you many projects to do so. We came from a mentoring and after school program for children who had nowhere to go after school, academic growth, access to counseling, tutor(s), meals/snacks, thanks to the financial support of my grandmother, Beatrice Herron, to what has become a clinically -sound practice accessible to the suburban and inner-city communities.

To God, who is the head of my life. You woke me up and gave me messages to the world during COVID that I could not video tape fast enough, so you told me to capture those messages for the year, and put them in a book! And I did!

NOTES

_____

_____

_____

_____

_____

_____

_____

_____

_____

_____

_____

NOTES

NOTES

_____

_____

_____

_____

_____

_____

_____

_____

_____

_____

_____

_____

www.ingramcontent.com/pod-product-compliance
Lightning Source LLC
Chambersburg PA
CBHW072207270326
41930CB00011B/2566